W9-AUI-528

sun + screen = sunscreen

Amanda Rondeau

Consulting Editor Monica Marx, M.A./Reading Specialist

Published by SandCastle™, an imprint of ABDO Publishing Company, 4940 Viking Drive, Edina, Minnesota 55435.

Printed in the United States.

Credits
Edited by: Pam Price
Curriculum Coordinator: Nancy Tuminelly
Cover and Interior Design and Production: Mighty Media
Photo Credits: BananaStock Ltd., Comstock, Corbis Images, Hemera, PhotoDisc, Rubberball Productions, Stockbyte

Library of Congress Cataloging-in-Publication Data

Rondeau, Amanda, 1974-
Sun + screen = sunscreen / Amanda Rondeau.
p. cm. -- (Compound words)
Includes index.
Summary: Illustrations and easy-to-read text introduce compound words related to travel.
ISBN 1-59197-440-2
1. English language--Compound words--Juvenile literature. [1. English language--Compound words.] I. Title.

PE1175 .R668 2003
428.1--dc21

2003048009

SandCastle™ books are created by a professional team of educators, reading specialists, and content developers around five essential components that include phonemic awareness, phonics, vocabulary, text comprehension, and fluency. All books are written, reviewed, and leveled for guided reading, early intervention reading, and Accelerated Reader® programs and designed for use in shared, guided, and independent reading and writing activities to support a balanced approach to literacy instruction.

Let Us Know

After reading the book, SandCastle would like you to tell us your stories about reading. What is your favorite page? Was there something hard that you needed help with? Share the ups and downs of learning to read. We want to hear from you! To get posted on the ABDO Publishing Company Web site, send us e-mail at:

sandcastle@abdopub.com

SandCastle Level: Transitional

A compound word is two words joined together to make a new word.

sun + screen =

sunscreen

Kyle's dad puts sunscreen on his face.

He doesn't want Kyle to get a sunburn.

suit + case =

suitcase

The Garcias are going to visit Aunt Emma.

They pack a suitcase and snacks for the drive.

sea + side =

seaside

Ella and her family take a trip to the seaside.

They like to play in the sand.

wind + mill =

windmill

Meg's family saw a windmill on their vacation.

tooth + paste =

toothpaste

Ana brings her
toothbrush and
toothpaste when
she goes to
Grandma's.

air + port =

airport

Morgan is at the airport.

She is going on vacation with her family.

No Need for Sunscreen

Grandma came for a visit
in the summertime.

She brought sunscreen,
but the sun didn't shine.

We were late because
of the rain, and we
rushed to meet
her airplane.

GRANDMA

Dad took the highway so we could get there in a hurry.

But Grandma took the subway
and hoped we would not worry.

We could not find her!

So we got home by nine.

We saw Grandma and her sunscreen made it just fine.

More Compound Words

airline
anywhere
crossroad
downtown
freeway
headlight
honeymoon
motorcycle
overpass
passport
poolside
postcard
railroad
runway
somewhere
timetable
tumbleweed
turnpike
uptown

Glossary

seaside	the land that borders the sea
subway	an electric railroad that runs underground in a city
sunburn	red, painful skin caused by staying in the sun too long
sunscreen	lotion that is used to protect the skin from the harmful rays of the sun
windmill	a machine powered by wind blowing against its vanes that is used to pump water, create electricity, or grind grain

About SandCastle™

A professional team of educators, reading specialists, and content developers created the SandCastle™ series to support young readers as they develop reading skills and strategies and increase their general knowledge. The SandCastle™ series has four levels that correspond to early literacy development in young children. The levels are provided to help teachers and parents select the appropriate books for young readers.

Emerging Readers
(no flags)

Beginning Readers
(1 flag)

Transitional Readers
(2 flags)

Fluent Readers
(3 flags)

These levels are meant only as a guide. All levels are subject to change.

To see a complete list of SandCastle™ books and other nonfiction titles from ABDO Publishing Company, visit **www.abdopub.com** or contact us at:

4940 Viking Drive, Edina, Minnesota 55435 • 1-800-800-1312 • fax: 1-952-831-1632